This book belongs to:
_____

Note to parents and carers

Many children are now taught to read using the phonic approach. This means they are taught to look at the letters, say the sounds, and then blend them to make a word. So, for example, children blend **c/a/t** to make the word **cat**, and **sh/o/p** to make **shop**.

When children have completed their initial phonics learning, they are ready to apply it to reading real books. Ladybird's **Superhero Phonic Readers** are planned for this exciting stage.

Some words are hard to read using beginner phonics. These words are often known as 'tricky words'. Some of these occur frequently in the English language so it is useful for children to memorize them.

Have fun doing our Tricky Words Memory Quiz on page 30. This features the most useful tricky words from the story.

How to use Superhero Phonic Readers:

⭐ Start at level one and gradually progress through the series. Each story is a little bit longer than the last and uses more grown-up vocabulary.

⭐ Children will be able to read **Superhero Phonic Readers** for themselves. Let your child read to you, and share the excitement!

⭐ If your child finds any words difficult, help him or her to work out the sounds in the word.

⭐ Early readers can be concentrating so hard on the words that they sometimes don't fully grasp the overall meaning of what they read. The puzzle questions on pages 28 and 29 will help with this. Have fun talking about them together.

⭐ There is a reward chart at the back of the book - young readers can fill this in and add stickers to it.

⭐ The Ladybird website **www.ladybird.com** features a wealth of information about phonics and reading.

⭐ Enjoy reading together!

Geraldine Taylor
Ladybird Educational Consultant

Educational Consultant: Geraldine Taylor

Phonics Consultant: Marj Newbury

A catalogue record for this book is available from the British Library

Published by Ladybird Books Ltd
80 Strand, London, WC2R 0RL
A Penguin Company

2 4 6 8 10 9 7 5 3 1
© LADYBIRD BOOKS LTD MMIX
LADYBIRD and the device of a Ladybird are trademarks of Ladybird Books Ltd

ISBN: 978-1-40930-260-5

Printed in Italy

Superhero Phonic Readers

Jumping Jade

written by Mandy Ross

illustrated by Mark Ruffle

Meet Jumping Jade. Jumping Jade can jump as high as a house. Or higher!

Jumping Jade likes to jump from roof to roof.
Do not do this at home, readers.

One day, Jumping Jade is jumping from roof to roof when she hears… nee-naw, nee-naw!

Jumping Jade can see police cars speeding to…

…the bank!

"A robber must be robbing the bank!" says Jade.

She hides behind a chimney to see. Police cars screech all around the bank.

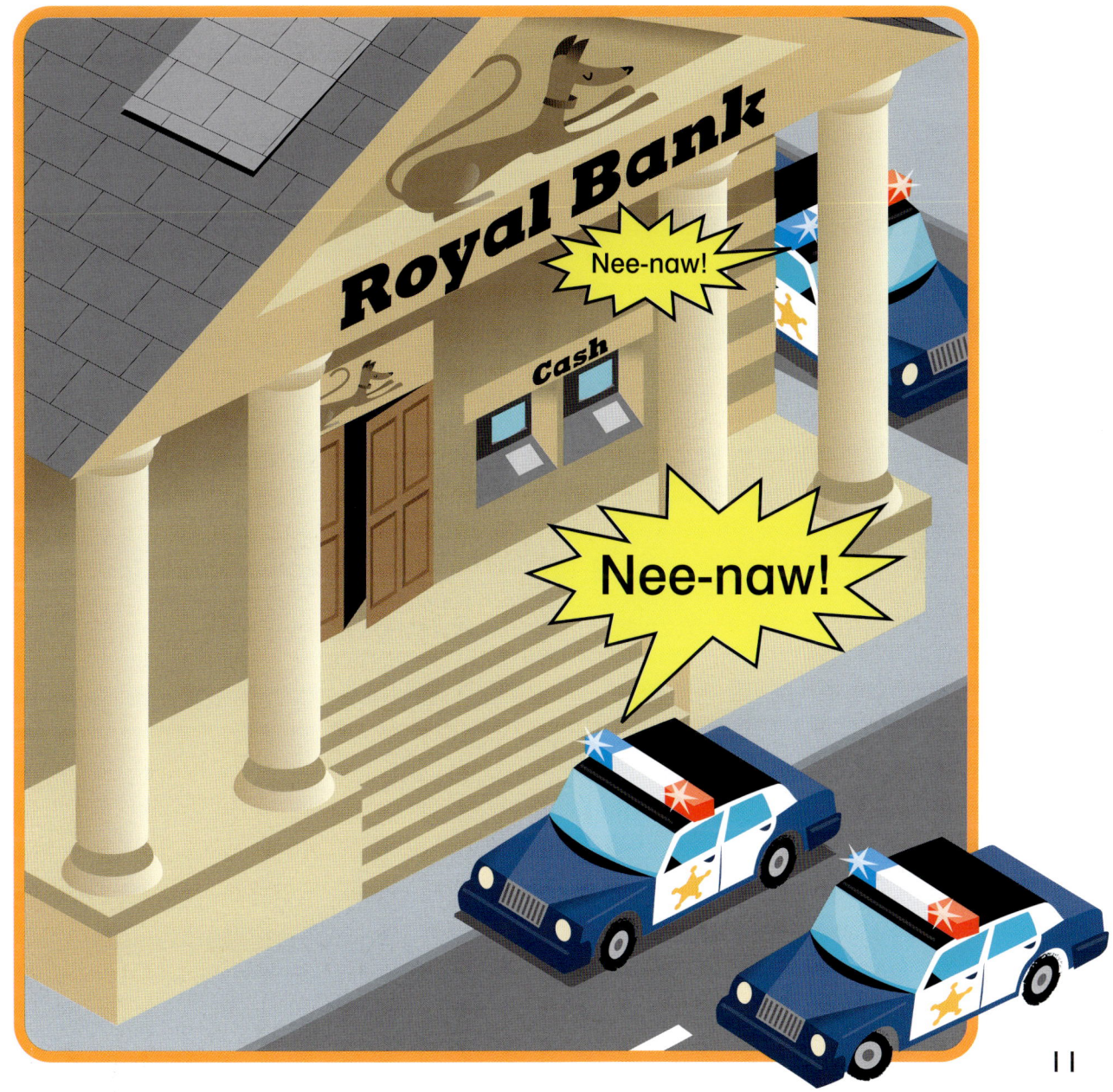

Jade can see from
behind the chimney.

Just then, a hatch opens on the roof of the bank.
Jade can see a hand. Out gets…

…Dax Doom!
"Look!" gasps Jumping Jade,
"he has a big sack of gold!"

Jumping Jade can see Dax Doom strapping on...

...a flying machine!

As Jade looks on, Dax Doom checks his straps. With a sneaky grin, he presses a button. The wings start to spin.

Just as the police get onto the roof, off zooms Dax Doom.

They see Dax Doom
zoom away.

"Oh, no!" puff the police.
"We have lost him!"

"Not so fast," says Jade. When Dax Doom flies near, she jumps!

Jade grabs Dax Doom and pulls him back down to the roof of…

…the jail! The police run all the way down the stairs of the bank.

They run all the way down the street.

They run all the way up the stairs and onto the roof of the jail.

"Good work, Jade!" puff the police.
Dax Doom is in handcuffs.

"Let me go!" he shouts as they take him down the stairs into the jail.

"Thanks, Jade," say the police.
"You helped us to catch Dax Doom."

And now Dax Doom is safely behind bars.
Or is he?

Superhero Secret Puzzles

⭐ What is Jade's super-power?

⭐ How does Jade know there is a bank-robber?

⭐ What does Jade hide behind?

⭐ How does Dax Doom get away from the police?

⭐ What is in Dax Doom's sack?

⭐ Where does Jade take Dax Doom?

⭐ How high can you jump?

Look at these pictures from the story and say the order they should go in.

A

B

C

D

Answer on page 30.

Tricky Words Memory Quiz

Can you remember these words from the story?

See if you can read them super-fast.

to
do
one
when
she
the
be
all
out
he

they
oh
no
we
have
so
work
me
go
into
you

What else can you remember?

Can you put the book down and say what happens in the story?

The answer to the picture puzzle on page 29 is: B, A, D, C.

I'm a phonic Superhero

I can read all of **Jumping Jade**.

I can read all the tricky words.

By _____

Date _____

level 3

I did great work

Well done!

I can read tricky words

I'm a phonics reader

I'm a reading hero

Jumping Jade

Dax Doom

Jumping Jade

Dax Doom

Jumping Jade